The Greatest Gift

The Story of Jesus and the Woman at the Well

We are grateful to the following team of authors for their contributions to *God Loves Me*, a Bible story program for young children. This Bible story, one of a series of fifty-two, was written by Patricia L. Nederveld, managing editor for CRC Publications. Suggestions for using this book were developed by Jesslyn DeBoer, a freelance author from Grand Rapids, Michigan. Yvonne Van Ee, an early childhood educator, served as project consultant and wrote *God Loves Me*, the program guide that accompanies this series of Bible storybooks.

Nederveld has served as a consultant to Title I early childhood programs in Colorado. She has extensive experience as a writer, teacher, and consultant for federally funded preschool, kindergarten, and early childhood programs in Colorado, Texas, Michigan, Florida, Missouri, and Washington, using the *High/Scope* Education Research Foundation curriculum. In addition to writing the *Bible Footprints* church curriculum for four- and five-year-olds, Nederveld edited the revised *Threes* curriculum and the first edition of preschool through second grade materials for the *LiFE* curriculum, all published by CRC Publications.

DeBoer has served as a church preschool leader and as coauthor of the preschool-kindergarten materials for the *LiFE* curriculum published by CRC Publications. She has also written K-6 science and health curriculum for Christian Schools International, Grand Rapids, Michigan, and inspirational gift books for Zondervan Publishing House.

Van Ee is a professor and early childhood program advisor in the Education Department at Calvin College, Grand Rapids, Michigan. She has served as curriculum author and consultant for Christian Schools International and wrote the original *Story Hour* organization manual and curriculum materials for fours and fives.

Photo on page 5: SuperStock; photo on page 20: Photodisc.

Library of Congress Cataloging-in-Publication Data

Nederveld, Patricia L., 1944-
     The greatest gift: the story of Jesus and the woman at the well/
Patricia L. Nederveld.
        p. cm. — (God loves me; bk. 30)
     Summary: A simple retelling of the story of at woman who gave Jesus
a drink of water and was rewarded with the gift of God's love.
Includes follow-up activities.
     ISBN 1-56212-299-1
     1. Samaritan woman (Biblical figure)—Juvenile literature.
2. Bible stories, English—N.T. John. 3. God—Love—Juvenile
literature. [1. Samaritan woman (Biblical figure). 2. Bible
stories—N.T.] I. Title. II. Series: Nederveld, Patricia L., 1944-
God loves me; bk. 30.
BS2520.S9N43   1998
232.9'.5—dc21

                           98-10843
                              CIP
                              AC

10 9 8 7 6 5 4 3 2 1

The Greatest Gift

The Story of Jesus and the Woman at the Well

PATRICIA L. NEDERVELD

ILLUSTRATIONS BY CATHY ANN JOHNSON

CRC Publications
Grand Rapids, Michigan

This is a story
from God's
book, the Bible.

It's for say name(s) of
your child(ren).
It's for me too!

John 4:3-30, 39-42

The sun was shining on Samaria. A woman walked along the hot, dusty road to the well. It was time to fill her empty jug with water.

A tired-looking stranger sat near the well. The woman wondered who he could be. "Will you give me a drink?" the tired stranger asked.

9

She did. What a wonderful gift for a thirsty stranger!

11

" I have a gift for you too!" said the stranger. "God loves you—that's the greatest gift of all! It's a gift for you—and for everyone who receives God's love."

" I know that God is going to send Jesus to us someday soon," said the woman. "I know that Jesus will teach us all about God's love!"

"I *am* Jesus," said the stranger with a smile.

Could it be true? Yes! The woman knew it was true. She left her water jar by the well and raced back home. She told the good news to everyone. "Quick! Come see Jesus!" she said.

Everyone crowded around Jesus. And Jesus told everyone about the greatest gift of all. "God loves you!" he said. Then everyone knew that Jesus was not a stranger. Jesus was God's own Son.

I wonder if you know that God loves you very much too . . .

Dear God, thank you for loving us so much. We're glad Jesus came to show us how much you love us. Amen.

Suggestions for Follow-up

Opening

Throughout your time together, look for opportunities to play or speak with each child individually. Your helpful hands, kind smile, and gentle words will express God's love for your little ones.

Bring a pitcher of ice water for your group time. Pour some of the water into a clear glass, and ask the children to tell you what's in the glass. Ask if they think it's hot or cold, and let them feel the water. Talk about how good cold water tastes on a hot day or after playtime. Put the pitcher and small paper cups in a spot where children can ask for a drink later. Explain that someone in your story today asked for a drink of water—wonder who that could be.

Learning Through Play

Learning through play is the best way! The following activity suggestions are meant to help you provide props and experiences that will invite the children to play their way into the Scripture story and its simple truth. Try to provide plenty of time for the children to choose their own activities and to play individually. Use group activities sparingly—little ones learn most comfortably with a minimum of structure.

1. Set up a "well" on the floor or low table. You will probably want to protect the area with newspapers or plastic and keep a mop handy. Old T-shirts or smocks will help keep your little ones dry. Use a large bucket for the well and tie a plastic cup to the handle with a long shoestring. Provide a supply of plastic containers of various sizes and shapes, and invite children to dip the cup into the water to draw water from the well to fill their containers. Ask children if this is the way they get a drink of water at their homes. Remind them that Jesus drank from a well, not from a faucet or drinking fountain like they do. You'll want to mention your own thankfulness to God for this wonderful gift as you talk about all the uses for water.

2. Provide water in small dishpans or plastic containers, and encourage children to wash dishes, wash doll clothes, give their babies a bath, cook with water, or scrub the floor. Be ready to wipe up excess spills, but let your little ones enjoy their work—and soap bubbles too. God gives us water every day for so many things, and God gives us *love* every day too!

3. Show the children the picture of the clay water jug the woman brought to the well. Then supply your little ones with Play-Doh and tell them clay is a lot like this. Invite them to shape it into a ball; then show them how to use their thumbs to make an indentation in the ball and how to use their thumbs and fingers to pinch the sides into a cup shape. Praise even their most lopsided efforts. As you pretend to drink from the cups, recall with the children how good a drink of cold water tastes on a hot day. It must have tasted good to Jesus too. Thank God for giving us refreshing water and for loving us so much.

4. Cut large water-glass shapes from white construction paper or posterboard. Provide 1" (2.5 cm) squares of light blue tissue paper or construction paper and glue sticks. Show your little ones how to glue the squares of paper to the glass to make a "water" collage as they pretend to fill the glass with water. As the children work, recall the woman's gift of water and Jesus' gift of God's love.

5. Let your little ones help you prepare a beverage for snack time. Emphasize that water is a wonderful gift from God as you fill small pitchers. Help the children measure lemonade mix and stir it into the water; then pour each child a cup to enjoy. Imagine together that you have been walking on a hot sunny day. As you and the children talk about how tired and thirsty you feel, ask if they remember who the thirsty stranger was. What did the woman give Jesus? What did Jesus give the woman?

Closing

Sing several of these stanzas of "God Is So Good" (Songs Section, *God Loves Me* program guide) as children follow your actions:

> *God is so good* . . . (point up)
> *He cares for me* . . . (point to self)
> *God loves me so* . . . (cross hands over heart)
> *Thank you, dear God* . . . (fold hands, sing prayer)
> —Words: Stanzas 1 and 2, traditional

At Home

Water, water everywhere! How many ways do you and your little one use water in your home each day? What about outdoors? How many places do you see water as you drive around your community? Water is a wonderful gift from God—and so is God's love! As you see and use water this week, count the ways, measure the amounts, and praise God for the gift of water and for the greatest gift of all.

Old Testament Stories

Blue and Green and Purple Too! *The Story of God's Colorful World*

It's a Noisy Place! *The Story of the First Creatures*

Adam and Eve *The Story of the First Man and Woman*

Take Good Care of My World! *The Story of Adam and Eve in the Garden*

A Very Sad Day *The Story of Adam and Eve's Disobedience*

A Rainy, Rainy Day *The Story of Noah*

Count the Stars! *The Story of God's Promise to Abraham and Sarah*

A Girl Named Rebekah *The Story of God's Answer to Abraham*

Two Coats for Joseph *The Story of Young Joseph*

Plenty to Eat *The Story of Joseph and His Brothers*

Safe in a Basket *The Story of Baby Moses*

I'll Do It! *The Story of Moses and the Burning Bush*

Safe at Last! *The Story of Moses and the Red Sea*

What Is It? *The Story of Manna in the Desert*

A Tall Wall *The Story of Jericho*

A Baby for Hannah *The Story of an Answered Prayer*

Samuel! Samuel! *The Story of God's Call to Samuel*

Lions and Bears! *The Story of David the Shepherd Boy*

David and the Giant *The Story of David and Goliath*

A Little Jar of Oil *The Story of Elisha and the Widow*

One, Two, Three, Four, Five, Six, Seven! *The Story of Elisha and Naaman*

A Big Fish Story *The Story of Jonah*

Lions, Lions! *The Story of Daniel*

New Testament Stories

Jesus Is Born! *The Story of Christmas*

Good News! *The Story of the Shepherds*

An Amazing Star! *The Story of the Wise Men*

Waiting, Waiting, Waiting! *The Story of Simeon and Anna*

Who Is This Child? *The Story of Jesus in the Temple*

Follow Me! *The Story of Jesus and His Twelve Helpers*

The Greatest Gift *The Story of Jesus and the Woman at the Well*

A Father's Wish *The Story of Jesus and a Little Boy*

Just Believe! *The Story of Jesus and a Little Girl*

Get Up and Walk! *The Story of Jesus and a Man Who Couldn't Walk*

A Little Lunch *The Story of Jesus and a Hungry Crowd*

A Scary Storm *The Story of Jesus and a Stormy Sea*

Thank You, Jesus! *The Story of Jesus and One Thankful Man*

A Wonderful Sight! *The Story of Jesus and a Man Who Couldn't See*

A Better Thing to Do *The Story of Jesus and Mary and Martha*

A Lost Lamb *The Story of the Good Shepherd*

Come to Me! *The Story of Jesus and the Children*

Have a Great Day! *The Story of Jesus and Zacchaeus*

I Love You, Jesus! *The Story of Mary's Gift to Jesus*

Hosanna! *The Story of Palm Sunday*

The Best Day Ever! *The Story of Easter*

Goodbye—for Now *The Story of Jesus' Return to Heaven*

A Prayer for Peter *The Story of Peter in Prison*

Sad Day, Happy Day! *The Story of Peter and Dorcas*

A New Friend *The Story of Paul's Conversion*

Over the Wall *The Story of Paul's Escape in a Basket*

A Song in the Night *The Story of Paul and Silas in Prison*

A Ride in the Night *The Story of Paul's Escape on Horseback*

The Shipwreck *The Story of Paul's Rescue at Sea*

Holiday Stories

Selected stories from the New Testament to help you celebrate the Christian year

Jesus Is Born! *The Story of Christmas*

Good News! *The Story of the Shepherds*

An Amazing Star! *The Story of the Wise Men*

Hosanna! *The Story of Palm Sunday*

The Best Day Ever! *The Story of Easter*

Goodbye—for Now *The Story of Jesus' Return to Heaven*

These fifty-two books are the heart of *God Loves Me*, a Bible story program designed for young children. Individual books (or the entire set) and the accompanying program guide *God Loves Me* are available from CRC Publications (1-800-333-8300).